D1391983

Books should be returned on or before the

Z 1215997   36 2·25

This book is due for return on or before the last date shown below.

Need to Know
Gambling

Michael Smeaton
and Paul Bellringer

Heinemann
LIBRARY

www.heinemann.co.uk/library

Visit our website to find out more information about **Heinemann Library** books.

To order:

☎ Phone 44 (0) 1865 888066
📄 Send a fax to 44 (0) 1865 314091
🖥 Visit the Heinemann Bookshop at www.heinemann.co.uk/library to browse our
catalogue and order online.

Produced by Roger Coote Publishing
Gissing's Farm, Fressingfield, Suffolk IP21 5SH, UK

First published in Great Britain by Heinemann
Library, Halley Court, Jordan Hill, Oxford OX2 8EJ,
part of Harcourt Education.
Heinemann is a registered trademark of Harcourt
Education Ltd.

Editorial: Katie Orchard
Design: Jane Hawkins
Picture Research: Lynda Lines
Production: Viv Hichens

Originated by Ambassador Litho Ltd
Printed and bound in China by
South China Printing Company

ISBN 0 431 09819 0
07 06 05 04 03
10 9 8 7 6 5 4 3 2 1

J362.25
Z1215997

British Library Cataloguing in Publication Data
Smeaton, Michael
Gambling. – (Need to know)
1.Gambling - Juvenile literature
I.Title II.Bellringer, Paul
362.2'5

Acknowledgements
The publishers would like to thank the following for
permission to reproduce photographs:
AKG London p. 11; Alamy Images p. 21 (Sindre
Ellingsen); British Museum, London p. 10; Camera
Press p. 12; Corbis pp. 9 (D Boone), 17 (Eye
Ubiquitous), 34 (Owen Franken), 43 (Layne
Kennedy); Digital Vision pp. 6, 7; Fokus/Niels Åge
Skovbo pp. 1, 28; Format Photographers p. 40
(Joanne O'Brien); Hodder Wayland Picture Library
p. 46; Impact p. 13 (Charles Coates); John Birdsall
Photography p. 32; Photofusion pp. 16 (Paul Doyle),
38 top (Gina Glover); Popperfoto pp. 4 (Reuters), 27
(Reuters), 31 (Reuters), 45 (Reuters), 47 (Reuters),
50; Rex Features *front cover* (Jeremy Sutton
Hibbert), pp. 5 (Jeremy Sutton Hibbert), 8 (Tim
Rooke), 15 (Ros Drinkwater), 18 (Nils Jorgensen),
19 (David Hurrell), 22 (Sipa/Andrew Holbrooke), 24
(IPC Images), 37 (Jeremy Sutton Hibbert), 38
bottom (Fotex/Melanie), 39 (Andrew Drysdale), 42
(Jeremy Sutton Hibbert), 49; Science Photo Library
p. 29 (Oscar Burrell); Topham Picturepoint p. 23
(Image Works/John Maier Jr.).

Every effort has been made to contact copyright
holders of any material reproduced in this book.
Any omissions will be rectified in subsequent
printings if notice is given to the publishers.

Any words appearing in the text in bold, **like this**,
are explained in the Glossary.

Contents

Gambling

'It could be you!' The UK public hears these words as they watch the television advertisements for the National **Lottery**. Every Saturday and Wednesday, right around the country, people queue up in droves at lottery counters in newsagent's and supermarkets to choose their 'lucky' numbers. As they wait for the draw, they dream of what they would do if they won the **jackpot**.

China has only recently lifted its ban on gambling activities and introduced a national lottery.

Meanwhile, at a Melbourne racecourse in Australia, thousands cheer as their horse heads off at the start of a race. The winners congratulate themselves for picking the first horse past the post, while the losers curse their luck and rip up their betting slips. In Texas, USA, a group of ladies meets up for their regular weekly **bingo** night, where they can catch up on the latest gossip with their friends, whilst marking their cards and hoping to beat the rest to a **full-house**. In the corner, someone uses the break between the games to have a quick go on the **slot machines** to try to hit the jackpot. It is late at a Monte Carlo **casino**, but there is an air of excitement as someone lays down a large bet on the **roulette** table. The wheel goes round and round as the crowd waits in anticipation of the possible 'big win' that could change someone's life for ever.

Gambling around us

All of these things are different types of gambling, which is used by many as a form of entertainment that may or may not bring them riches. It gives us highs and lows, suspense, excitement and fun, and can be done alone or together with a group of friends. For some people, gambling is about winning the 'big one' and becoming richer than their wildest dreams. For others it is about beating the **odds** and feeling good just to have won, no matter how small the amount. Whatever the reasons may be for gambling, it is now enjoyed by the majority of the population in one form or another, and is available in almost every town and city around the world. Gambling is an integral part of our lives and the entertainment industry, and for most people it is just a bit of harmless fun. But not everyone can control their gambling.

❝❝I will never forget the excitement that I felt every time I walked into the arcade. I fell in love with the noise, the lights and the buzz. Before I knew it, I was hooked.❞❞

(Michael, aged nineteen)

The glamour of casinos and the chance to win large amounts of money are major attractions for customers.

What is gambling?

Gambling is a form of risk-taking. Some people argue that we all gamble to some extent – crossing the road or taking part in certain extreme physical sports are all activities that involve risk. Risk-taking is part of human nature, and the greater the risk, the more excitement we feel. There are many different types of gambling, and most people who gamble have their own favourite (see pages 8–9), but most gambling activities share the same basic elements.

Placing the bet

Any gambling activity must involve at least two people. This may be between two friends who are betting against each other on the outcome of an event, such as the toss of a coin or the result of a football game. It may also be between an individual and a gambling **operator**, such as a **bookmaker** or **slot-machine** operator.

The stake

Gambling always involves a **stake** that is passed on from the loser to the winner. A stake is whatever the gambler is prepared to risk to win the bet. In most cases the stake is usually money, although other objects of value have been used to cover a bet.

People that take part in extreme sports get a rush of excitement from the risk involved. This can be similar to the 'buzz' some gamblers feel.

The uncertain outcome

A central part of gambling is that the outcome of the bet has to be uncertain. If the outcome was known then there would be no risk, or excitement, to the activity. The result of a gamble must be determined (at least partly) by chance. Some activities involve nothing but luck, such as **roulette** or the **lottery**, where gamblers have no way of influencing the result. Others, such as card playing, allow a gambler to use their skill to influence the outcome. A professional card player can keep track of the cards or influence other players, and improve their chances of winning. However, there is still an element of luck involved in the cards that are dealt to players.

Whilst many gamblers use **form guides** to select the most likely dog to win a race, many just pick a name that they like or choose at random.

Playing for high stakes

In 1777, Robert Coleman and Baron Harry W. Stiegal were two of the most successful businessmen in Pennsylvania, USA. They often played cards together for moderate stakes. Slowly the stakes got bigger and bigger. When Baron Stiegal's money ran out, he began using other assets as stakes. Over time Coleman managed to win Stiegal's stallions, waterworks, warehouses and most other properties that he had worked years to obtain.

What is gambling?

A sporting bet

One of the most popular forms of gambling is betting. This generally involves placing a bet on a sporting event at a bookmaker's – horse racing is the most popular event. The amount an individual can win depends on the amount staked and the **odds** (probability) of that horse winning. Other events that are popular with gamblers include dog racing and football.

Betting machines

Another popular gambling activity is playing on **fruit machines**, also known as slot machines or one-armed bandits. There are also similar gambling games in Australia called **pokies** (video poker machines).

Casino games

Casinos have the greatest variety of games available in one venue. As well as playing on high-**jackpot** slot machines, gamblers can play various card games for money, such as poker and **blackjack**, try their hand at **craps**, or take a chance on the roulette table. Casinos differ from other gambling venues because gambling chips are used instead of money. These are small, coloured discs, each with a different monetary value. Gamblers purchase the chips in the casino in order to gamble on the tables.

High street betting offices give odds on all kinds of sporting events.

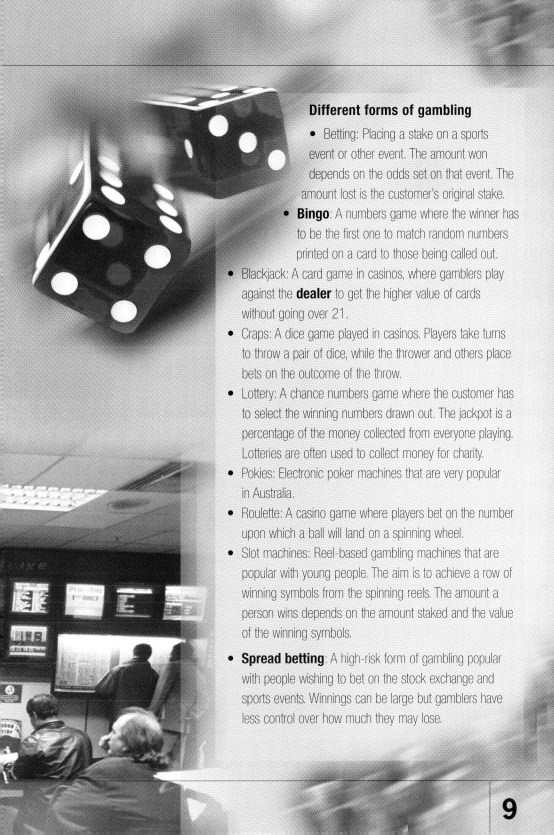

Different forms of gambling

- Betting: Placing a stake on a sports event or other event. The amount won depends on the odds set on that event. The amount lost is the customer's original stake.
- **Bingo**: A numbers game where the winner has to be the first one to match random numbers printed on a card to those being called out.
- Blackjack: A card game in casinos, where gamblers play against the **dealer** to get the higher value of cards without going over 21.
- Craps: A dice game played in casinos. Players take turns to throw a pair of dice, while the thrower and others place bets on the outcome of the throw.
- Lottery: A chance numbers game where the customer has to select the winning numbers drawn out. The jackpot is a percentage of the money collected from everyone playing. Lotteries are often used to collect money for charity.
- Pokies: Electronic poker machines that are very popular in Australia.
- Roulette: A casino game where players bet on the number upon which a ball will land on a spinning wheel.
- Slot machines: Reel-based gambling machines that are popular with young people. The aim is to achieve a row of winning symbols from the spinning reels. The amount a person wins depends on the amount staked and the value of the winning symbols.
- **Spread betting**: A high-risk form of gambling popular with people wishing to bet on the stock exchange and sports events. Winnings can be large but gamblers have less control over how much they may lose.

History of gambling

Throughout recorded history, fortunes have been won or lost through gambling – homes, wives, slaves and even lives have been lost. There is evidence from 2000 BCE that the Egyptians played games of chance with knuckle-bones painted as four-sided dice. In China, around 1500 BCE, people used spinning disks to play a gambling game similar to **roulette**. Ancient Greek and Roman nobles visited health spas to rest their bodies and play games, many of which were gambling activities. In 210 CE the first recorded horserace in England took place and there is little doubt that money was **staked** on the outcome.

Society has always had an uneasy relationship with gambling, and the practice has often swung in and out of favour. In England, for example, in 1388, King Charles II passed a law making it illegal for men to play dice, quoits or tennis (all betting games) on a Sunday. However, exactly 200 years later, Queen Elizabeth I encouraged gambling when she approved the first **lottery** in order to help pay for the upkeep of the Cinque Ports. Society's constantly changing attitude to gambling and its acceptability has been reflected worldwide.

Like the Ancient Egyptians, the Ancient Greeks gambled with knuckle-bones.

Early casinos

In 1626, Venice, in Italy, opened the first legal public gambling house. Soon members of high society began to meet in such places, called 'little-houses', or *casini*, to talk politics, do business or gamble. Gambling houses spread throughout Europe and were patronized by the rich and fashionable aristocracy. Gambling became an organized, legal activity, with **casinos** thriving in England, France and Germany. Casinos soon gained a reputation as places of **vice** and excess, where fortunes could be made and lost overnight, and lives could be ruined or changed forever on the outcome of a hand of cards.

Into modern times

Because of its reputation for sending people to financial ruin, gambling has often been the subject of heated moral debate. However, by the 20th century, the activity had become slightly more acceptable as a tolerated vice. Today it is regarded as a normal leisure activity, and is found in almost every town or city around the world.

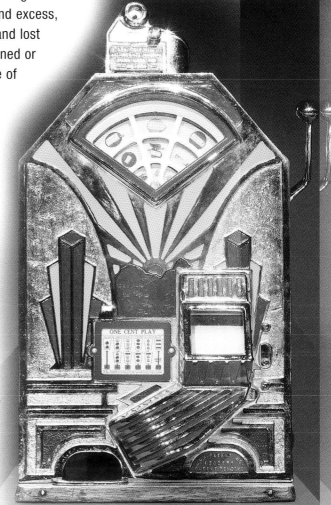

One-armed bandits (early slot machines) have been around since 1895. This one was made in the USA in 1932.

The big attraction

Today, gambling is one of the most popular forms of entertainment and it is available in most societies around the world. It appeals to people of all ages and backgrounds: young and old, male and female, and rich and poor. But what makes it so attractive?

The 'buzz' of gambling

On a human level, gambling is appealing because it is an activity that contains risk. Many gamblers feel that the excitement and 'buzz' of gambling comes from not knowing whether they will win or lose. The risk and uncertainty adds to the entertainment, and makes gambling even more enjoyable when a person wins.

Winning money

One of the major attractions of gambling comes from the possibility of winning money – whether it is a couple of pounds from a **slot machine** or a million-pound **jackpot**. National or state-run **lotteries** certainly raise the appeal of gambling by giving customers the opportunity to win millions. However, the chances of actually winning the top prize are

In Japan, *pachinko* is a gambling game that is popular with people of all ages.

Gamblers at the racecourse in Calcutta, India, anxiously look on as the horses gallop towards the finish.

incredibly low – for example, the chances of winning the UK National Lottery jackpot are 14 million to one. For most people, becoming a millionaire is just a distant dream.

Winning even a small amount of money can give the gambler more than just a bit of extra pocket money. Some gambling activities involve an element of problem solving, such as studying **form guides** for horses or football (working out the most likely outcome based on a horse's or team's past performance). Winning a bet from problem solving makes the gambler feel good about their 'skills' and abilities.

Escaping reality

Some gambling venues allow the individual to feel that they are escaping reality. **Casinos**, **amusement arcades**, **bookmakers** and **bingo** halls all provide an environment where the individual can become immersed in the atmosphere, losing themselves in a fantasy world. They are places where the gambler can forget about any negative feelings they may have in their life and become absorbed in the excitement of gambling.

The excitement, chance of winning, ability to escape and wide availability of gambling opportunities make gambling a very attractive form of entertainment. Whether people do it to try to make money, to liven up a football match, or simply to try to beat the **odds** and feel a sense of achievement, many find the pull of gambling irresistible.

Attitudes to gambling

Gambling has always been a subject of controversy. While many people object to gambling, many others feel that it is just a form of entertainment. Because of the popularity of gambling, and the fact that it can generate huge revenues for governments and **operators**, there has had to be some compromise.

Government attitudes

Many governments have decided to relax laws on certain gambling activities in order to be able to generate an income from them. In the UK, for example, **off-course betting** (placing bets with unofficial operators outside racecourses) was illegal before 1960. However, it proved impossible to prevent off-course betting from taking place, so the government decided to legalize the now commonplace **betting office**. This gave the government more control over gambling activities and also generated a tax revenue from legal betting offices.

However, it is clear that society's uneasy relationship with gambling has not entirely disappeared. In the USA, the government is discussing the **prohibition** of Internet gambling. In Australia, where there is a high **prevalence** of problem gambling, the government has recently decided to restrict the growth of '**pokie**' (video poker) machines. New Zealand has recently announced a halt on the opening of more **casinos**.

Another fear that governments have about gambling is that as a cash-generating business it is, unless tightly controlled, likely to attract cheats. One recent example of this in the UK

> **❝There is not a prison or house of correction in London which does not every day furnish abundant and conclusive testimony of the vast number of youths who are led into crime by the temptation of gaming establishments.❞**
>
> (Sir Alexander Cockburn, UK Attorney General, 1853)

concerned **spread betting**. **Odds** were offered on how many seconds would pass before the first throw-in of a professional football match. Those involved in the scam placed bets to say it would occur in the first few seconds after kick-off, and conspired with some of the footballers to make sure the ball was kicked out of play immediately after the whistle was blown.

Gambling and religion

Many religious faiths have found gambling easy to condemn but difficult to stop. For example, the Qu'ran expressly forbids gambling activities of any kind, yet large numbers of Muslims can be seen at gambling venues around the world.

The Christian Church has also been contradictory, disapproving of gambling from the pulpit only to hold fundraising **bingo** events and raffles in church halls.

The **Mormons** consider gambling to be morally wrong, yet they played a part in setting up and establishing some casinos in Las Vegas, in the USA.

Las Vegas is the gambling capital of the world. It is seen by many as the most exciting place to gamble.

Where do people gamble?

Gambling is all around us. It is almost impossible to walk around a town or city without coming across some form of gambling activity.

Traditional venues

At racecourses, people can place bets on horse and greyhound races. These races are also beamed to screens in **bookmaker's**, where gamblers can bet on them without venturing to the race track. Bookmakers also offer the chance to bet on other sporting events, such as football and cricket matches, as well as election results or even whether it will

snow at Christmas! Many towns and cities have **casinos**, where people can play card games, **roulette**, **craps** and **slot machines** with large jackpots. At some casinos with an elite clientele, some card tables will not accept bets of less than £20,000 a hand.

Bingo halls are now popular gambling venues, especially in the UK. People go there to socialize with friends and try their luck.

Bingo halls are becoming popular. Although traditionally an activity for older people, bingo is now becoming more attractive to young adults. Bingo is seen as a more sociable form of gambling – many people go to bingo halls with their friends. As well as regular bingo games with various prizes there is usually a selection of slot machines.

Amusement arcades are very popular in seaside towns but are also present in most towns and cities. These arcades contain slot machines, **pokie** machines and often other arcade games as well. Arcades are the most popular venues for younger gamblers.

High Street gambling

Gambling does not just take place in dedicated gambling venues. Many newsagent's and supermarkets around the world now sell **scratch cards** and **lottery** tickets. Pubs, bars and social clubs often have slot machines. In Australia a person can walk into a bar and play on pokie machines, place a bet on a race, or try their luck with a numbers game called **keno** (a lottery-style game), which is beamed out by a casino every five minutes. Cafés, leisure centres, cinemas, railway

stations, airports, and even cruise ships and ferries now have slot machines. Of course, if there is not a local gambling opportunity, individuals can still gamble by placing private bets with their friends. If a person wishes to gamble, there will always be an opportunity to do so.

Money raised from lottery tickets is often used by the government to supplement national services.

Where do people gamble?

The changing face of gambling

In the last few years, the face of gambling has changed dramatically. Developments in technology have enabled society to gain access to new forms of gambling. The Internet has led to a massive growth in gambling opportunities, allowing the customer to have access to **e-gaming platforms** 24 hours a day from the comfort of their own homes. Players can now gamble in **virtual casinos**, where they can play card games, roulette and even slot machines through their computer screens.

Bookmakers have set up Internet sites to allow customers to place bets on any sport they wish, from anywhere in the world. Customers can also play bingo, lotteries, and even bet on virtual snail races.

Internet gambling brings casino games straight into people's homes.

The development of digital television will soon allow individuals to use the television for more than just watching programmes. Technology is being developed to allow customers to place bets on live sports events shown on television, by using their remote controls. This technology can also be used to show live **casino** games and place bets on them. People no longer have to visit a bookmaker's or a casino if they want to gamble. The customer can now do these things with the touch of a button, from their own lounge or bedroom.

What is the future?

As new technology develops, so will new opportunities to gamble. The mobile phone can now be used to place bets and, as the phones become more powerful, more gambling activities will become available through them. Who knows what will be possible in five years' time?

Whilst the development of new gambling opportunities is good in terms of being more convenient for the customer, there may also be a negative side. Some people fear that an

People surfing the Internet will almost certainly be bombarded with adverts for e-gaming platforms.

increase in gambling opportunities may cause an increase in the numbers of people with gambling problems. Others are concerned about the security of gambling sites (where gamblers have to give credit card details), and whether customers will receive their winnings. Whatever the good points and bad points, one thing is for certain – gambling will always be with us, in one form or another.

Who gambles?

So, who gambles? The answer is most of us. In all the countries where gambling is widely available, between 65 per cent and 90 per cent of the adult population will gamble on one or more activity. The most popular form of gambling is playing the **lottery**, but **casino** betting and **slot machines** all have a strong following. There are also many other gambling opportunities on the High Street, over the telephone or via **e-gaming platforms**. The range of the population that participates in these activities is very broad.

Age seems to be an important factor in determining an individual's preferred gambling activity. In most countries, the age at which a person is allowed to gamble is defined by national or **federal law** (see pages 44–45), so gambling is mostly seen as an adult activity. The UK, however, is the only country in western Europe that allows children of any age to play on what are called 'Amusement with Prizes' machines (better known as slot or **fruit machines**). This is also the most popular gambling activity for young people around the world.

From the age of 25 upwards, betting at a **bookmaker's** and playing casino table games begin to be more popular gambling activities. Running across the different age groups is the interest in lotteries. In many countries, statistics show that for the older generations, particularly women, **bingo** is the preferred form of gambling – partly, it is suggested, because of the fact that it provides a social club for people with time on their hands.

Men are still more likely than women to be seen in a **betting office**. However, the number of female gamblers is increasing slowly.

There is a popular view that men gamble a great deal more than women. In some countries that is true, but in the UK the percentage difference between the sexes is quite small. In 2000, a national survey of the UK showed that 76 per cent of men gamble, compared to 68 per cent of women. However, a number of online gambling websites, especially those with a high percentage of US customers, have reported a higher percentage of women visiting the sites, compared to men.

The gambling industry

Gambling is big business. At the last count (1998) it was estimated that in the UK alone a staggering £7.5 billion was spent on gambling. This means that, on average, £20 million was spent every day. In Australia, a country with a high spend per person on gambling and just one-third of the UK population, the annual spend was around A$12.4 billion (£4.4 billion).

There are really only two big winners from gambling – the first is obviously the **operator** (the organization or person running the gambling activity), as the **odds** for winning are always in their favour, and the second is the government. One of the major reasons why many governments support the gambling industry is because they can earn a significant amount of money from taxing it.

A tax on dreams?

Governments strapped for cash and with a range of priorities to deal with are tempted to go for whatever help is available. **Lotteries** have been dubbed by some as 'a tax on dreams' because they are seen as a means of raising additional money to pay for services and development in many countries around the world. In the USA, the government was faced

Some of the world's biggest casinos are in Las Vegas, USA.

with the problem of improving conditions in the North American Indian **reservations** – often places with high unemployment and low morale. The federal governments allowed each state to give special concessions to these reservations so that they could develop **casinos** and other gambling activities. The money raised by the gambling industry went towards much needed health and education projects in the reservations. In many cases, this policy has been very successful. Another US example is Atlantic City, an area that had a reputation for being poor and run-down. Massive resort-style casinos were developed in the city and this investment has been seen to improve the quality of life for the people who live there.

The average amount spent on gambling per person each year

Australia	£240/A$685
UK	£130/A$370
US	£125/A$355
New Zealand	£85/A$240

(Source: *BISL 2000 – The economic value and public perceptions of gambling in the UK*)

Casinos in North American reservations such as this one have proved a popular way of generating income for the community.

What is problem gambling?

Most people enjoy gambling as a harmless bit of fun. However, for some people it can develop into a serious **addiction**, destroying the lives of the gamblers and their families.

The official definition

Just like drinking and taking drugs, gambling is an activity that can take over an individual's life. However, gambling has not always been seen as a true addiction. One key reason for this is that gamblers are not addicted to a substance such as nicotine in cigarettes, alcohol, or various other drugs. The **addictive** nature of gambling is mainly based around the activity forming a 'mental' or '**psychological**' addiction for the gambler.

In 1980, addiction to gambling was officially recognized as a **mental disorder** by the American Psychiatric Association. A list of criteria was drawn up to help counsellors and psychiatrists decide if an individual has a gambling addiction. This list is known as the DSM-IV Criteria for **Pathological** Gambling. This list is now used all over the world to help decide how bad a person's gambling problem is.

For some people gambling can turn into an all-consuming, destructive addiction.

DSM-IV Criteria for Pathological Gambling

The DSM-IV Criteria is a list of nine statements that describe the behaviour of a gambler. An individual has a serious gambling problem if their behaviour matches at least four of the statements on the list. The wording of the statements is complex, but can be summed up as follows:

- a greater **preoccupation** with gambling over time;
- a need to gamble with more and more money to maintain excitement;
- becoming restless or irritated when cutting down or stopping gambling;
- gambling to escape from problems;
- returning to gambling in order to win back money that has been lost;
- lying to family and friends to hide the amount of gambling;
- committing crime in order to obtain money for gambling;
- risking a job, relationship or education because of gambling;
- borrowing money in order to gamble or pay off gambling debts.

What is problem gambling?

Social gamblers

There can be a fine line between being a social gambler who enjoys gambling without developing a problem, and a problem gambler whose gambling takes over their life. Some social gamblers may even spend more money than problem gamblers, but do not go on to develop a problem.

Problem gamblers

There are three main factors that help determine those who are social gamblers from those who have a serious problem or are at risk of developing one. The first of these is being unable to stop. It is important that a gambler knows when to stop gambling – whether they are winning or losing. Social gamblers will be able to win or lose a bet and walk away, but problem gamblers will carry on gambling regardless. Even when they know they should stop gambling they are unable to pull themselves away from the activity.

The second sign of a gambling problem is that the urge to gamble overrides all other considerations. A problem gambler's life revolves around gambling. Other activities that

they once enjoyed – such as sports, education and relationships – will become discarded. Young problem gamblers often gamble instead of going to school, risking their education and friendships.

The third sign of a gambling addiction is when a person becomes hooked on the 'high' that is experienced when gambling. Problem gamblers often describe this feeling as a 'buzz'. It is the risk and excitement of gambling that gives them this buzz, and they are unable to experience this feeling in any other activity.

"I was not sleeping at night while I was gambling, because I was thinking about where I was going to get money from tomorrow."

(Anonymous problem gambler)

Excessive gambling

Many people believe that a gambling **addict** gambles because of greed. While it is true that gambling gives people the opportunity to win money, most of the time gamblers lose. Problem gamblers certainly want to win money, but only so that they have enough money to continue gambling. It is the activity itself that they are addicted to. Problem gamblers find that their gambling fulfils three basic needs: escape, power and action.

Escape

Problem gamblers are often vulnerable people – those who feel isolated from society in some way, or who have personal or money problems. The gambling environment provides some people with an escape from reality. **Amusement arcades** are a good example: while playing on a **slot machine**, problem gamblers can shut out all the negative feelings in their head. They become totally absorbed in what they are doing and wish only to be able to stay in that environment for as long as possible.

Some gamblers are desperate to win money so that they can continue to spend it on gambling for longer periods.

Power

Some gamblers feel that they are not in control of their day-to-day life. They believe that gambling gives them back some control and a sense of achievement. The challenge of beating the **odds** becomes an **obsession**. The need to feel powerful is especially relevant to young people who want to feel good at something. Young gamblers often boast about their skills at playing on **fruit machines.**

Action

The need for the 'buzz' associated with taking a risk is a powerful urge for some people. Gambling on fruit machines in particular becomes an activity where people feel this excitement. But money problems start when people have to risk more and more money in order to keep the 'buzz' going.

How big is the problem?

Studies over the last few years have tended to focus on the percentage of problem gamblers in the whole adult population, rather than just among those that gamble. As can be seen from the fact box, Australia appears to have the greatest **prevalence** of problem gambling, and Sweden has the lowest. The 0.8 per cent figure for the UK represents in the region of 350,000 problem gamblers. This figure, however, does not include the number of people – including family and friends – who are affected by the problem gambler.

In most cases men will gamble more than women, although, as has been highlighted on page 21, in the UK the difference is not great. The divide between the sexes is much greater, however, for those with a gambling problem. Men are three times more likely than women to become problem gamblers.

When it comes to age, younger gamblers are, without doubt, the most vulnerable group. This has been known for a long time and is one reason why some countries and states ban those under 21 or even under 25 from some gambling activities. An interesting pattern emerges when age is related to activity. Young gamblers love the **slot** and **pokie** machines, those in their mid-twenties to their forties prefer betting and **casino** table games, and the older generations tend to prefer the **lottery** and **bingo**. The pattern of problem gambling tends to mirror this trend. The UK National Gambling Helpline statistics for the year 2000 recorded that over 80 per cent of calls by those under 25 were about a problem with **slot machines** and 60 per cent of problem gamblers aged 36–45 involved betting.

However, these differences between problem gamblers' preferred gambling activities are rapidly becoming blurred. People are now getting into serious difficulty with a range of gambling activities – probably caused by the arrival of **e-gaming platforms** and a global mix of gambling opportunities.

Percentage of adults with a gambling problem

Australia	2.3%
Spain	1.4%
New Zealand	1.2%
USA	1.1%
United Kingdom	0.8%
Sweden	0.6%

(Source: *Gambling Behaviour in Britain: Results from the British Gambling Prevalence Survey, 2000*)

Horse races such as the Melbourne Cup, in Australia, are major sporting events, with large sums of money being won and lost on the day.

Gambling and young people

Is it fair that access to gambling is denied young people because a minority of them could get into trouble? Many young people may feel that it is very definitely unfair. However, statistics show that the younger a person is when they start gambling, the more likely they will be to develop a gambling problem.

Gambling is particularly attractive to young people because it seems fun, exciting, sociable, risky, daring and glamorous. It can make a person feel good, give them a buzz, make them feel powerful, and allow them to escape from day-to-day **anxieties**. Some young people feel that through gambling they can gain status, either by boasting about winning, or appearing to be 'cool' when they lose. From early teens upwards, it is normal for young people to want to face certain 'rites of passage' to quickly become an 'adult'. Gambling falls into the list of activities that many teenagers feel have to be tried, but it has to be treated with great respect.

The risk of developing a problem

In 2000, there was a **prevalence** study in the UK looking at gambling behaviour. The report uncovered a very telling figure that highlights the risk to young people. When people with a gambling problem were broken down into age groups, the highest prevalence of problem gambling was within the age group of males aged between 16 and 24 years old. The percentage of those that had gambled in 1999 who had a serious gambling problem was 4 per cent, which is far higher than the percentage of problem gamblers in the other age groups.

Young people are more vulnerable and more likely than adults to develop a gambling problem. Most forms of gambling are illegal for people under the age of eighteen. This is mainly due to the possible financial costs of gambling, and the maturity and responsibility needed to control gambling behaviour. The younger a person begins gambling, the more likely they will be to develop a gambling problem. While young people are not going to stop gambling, it is important that they are made aware of the possible risks involved and are equipped with the knowledge that will enable them to gamble responsibly.

Gambling on fruit machines is especially popular with young people, and it is one of the most addictive forms of gambling.

Warning signs

Alcoholics or drug **addicts** usually display certain physical symptoms that may alert other people to the fact that there is a problem – such as **disorientation**, discoloured skin or dilated pupils. This is quite important as it allows family and friends to identify the problem and possibly assist that individual in tackling their **addiction**. One reason why problem gambling is a dangerous addiction is that it is easily disguised and may go unnoticed by friends and family members for a long time.

The hidden addiction

Because gambling addicts do not really show any obvious physical symptoms, problem gambling is often referred to as the 'hidden addiction'. There are many other reasons why it is difficult to know if someone has a gambling problem, a few of which are listed below:

- gamblers often do not believe that they have a problem;
- problem gamblers become very good at hiding the truth about their gambling from others;
- money shortages and debts are quite easy to explain;
- gambling may be only one of several excessive behaviours;
- problem gamblers keep their gambling to themselves and will usually gamble alone, outside their social circle.

As with any addiction, the longer a gambling problem continues, the more destructive it may become. It is important to identify the addiction early so that the individual can get help as soon as possible.

What to look for

There are a few signs and symptoms that may point towards a person having a gambling problem. These include a high level of knowledge about gambling; constantly having pockets full of coins or tokens; a lack of hobbies or interests; a decline in quality of schoolwork; truancy or work **absenteeism**; mood swings and restlessness; frequent requests to borrow money from friends; and always being short of money. Many young people may display some of this behaviour without there being a problem at all. However, when a lot of the behaviour is seen together, it could suggest that a gambling problem exists.

Money problems are a common factor with gambling addicts. Problem gamblers often have to borrow money to fund their habit.

Living with problem gambling

The **psychological** effects of gambling on an individual and those around them can be devastating. For a problem gambler, feeding their **addiction** becomes the most important thing – the only thing – in their lives. The complete **preoccupation** with gambling may lead a problem gambler to neglect other important parts of their life. School or work may no longer seem important, and time that should be spent studying or working is used to gamble instead.

Lies and deceit

Gambling **addicts** become very good liars, hiding their destructive gambling and crippling debts from those around them, and even from themselves. They become skilled at making up believable stories about what they have been spending their time doing, or why they are short of money. As the need for money becomes greater, so do the lies and deceit that the gambler uses in order to borrow money from others, or to convince others that they do not have a problem.

> **"I used to tell ... lie after lie, and all for the sake of a bet."**
>
> **(Anonymous serving prisoner, aged 32)**

Debt and crime

The need to continue gambling at any cost will often lead a problem gambler to take desperate measures to fund their habit. Gambling can be a very expensive addiction, and gambling debts can spiral out of control. Committing crime is a common occurence for gambling addicts as they struggle to control their finances and feed their habit.

Negative thoughts

The build up of lies, criminal activity and self-neglect takes a heavy toll on the gambler. Whilst on the outside they may appear happy, that is usually a mask to cover up their torment. Problem gamblers can become depressed and withdrawn, with their minds dominated by negative feelings. This increases their urge to gamble, as it is the only activity they know that will help them escape from these

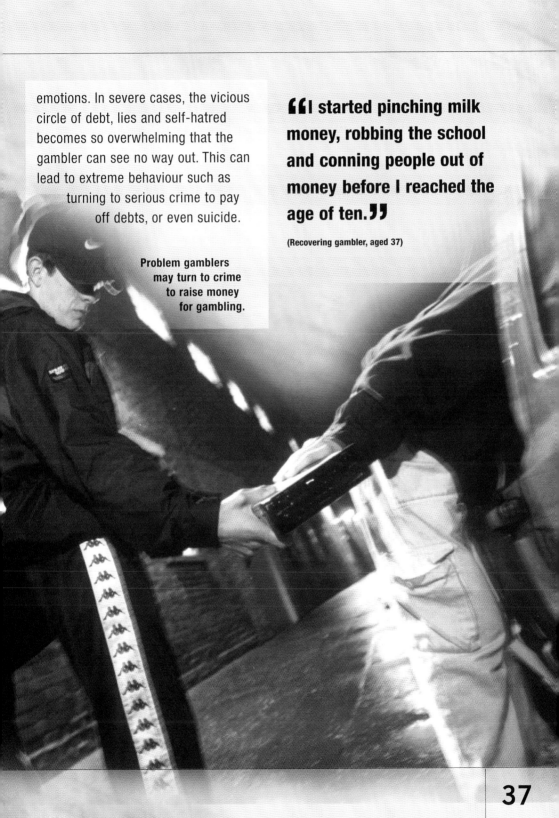

emotions. In severe cases, the vicious circle of debt, lies and self-hatred becomes so overwhelming that the gambler can see no way out. This can lead to extreme behaviour such as turning to serious crime to pay off debts, or even suicide.

Problem gamblers may turn to crime to raise money for gambling.

❝I started pinching milk money, robbing the school and conning people out of money before I reached the age of ten.❞

(Recovering gambler, aged 37)

Living with problem gambling

Impact on the family

The impact of a gambling addict on those around them can be very far reaching. In the case of an adult gambler, it has been suggested that their problem can affect as many as fifteen people, including family, friends, work colleagues and employers.

The impact of an adult problem gambler on their family can be particularly devastating. Because a problem gambler tends to hide the extent of their gambling and their debts, they can often lead the whole family into a financial crisis. In severe cases, gambling addicts may lose all their belongings, including their family home, because of gambling debts. Such stress can often lead to arguments within the family. Marriage breakdowns and divorces are common with problem gamblers.

Children can be directly affected by the tension and money worries within the home. Money shortages and the preoccupation with gambling can also lead to neglect of a child's basic needs, such as food, love and security. Many parents who are gambling addicts have been known to leave their children alone in a house or a car whilst they gamble.

Funding the habit

Young and old problem gamblers often seek opportunities to obtain more money to fund their gambling. Family, friends, work colleagues and employers of problem gamblers may find themselves victims of crime. Whether it is through direct stealing or borrowing money without returning it, those close to a gambler are easy targets. Problem gamblers also tend to find themselves jobs that in some way involve handling money, which becomes another source of income for their gambling.

❝❝I stole my daughter's television to fund my gambling. I paid £200 originally for the television, and got £50 for it from a second-hand dealer. Then I spent that £50 in the afternoon [on gambling], and it was all gone.❞❞

(Anonymous problem gambler)

People affected by a problem gambler

- The gambler's partner
- The gambler's children
- The gambler's parents
- The partner's parents
- The gambler's employer
- The gambler's work colleagues
- The gambler's friends and relations
- Small businesses
- State resources (police resources, social services and prisons)

Tim's story

Tim was sixteen when he started gambling on **fruit machines** regularly. As a child he remembers going to seaside **amusement arcades** and being excited by the lights and noise, but he never gambled. It was when he went to an arcade one day with a friend that his journey into gambling addiction began.

At the time, Tim was a bit depressed. His brothers had left home to go to university, and he was getting fed up with the pressure from his schoolwork. He remembers how he got quite excited the first time he gambled with his friend, especially when he won. For a while, Tim had forgotten about his troubles and felt a sense of achievement and power. From that moment he made a point of visiting the arcade to gamble whenever he went shopping on his own. Soon he would make special trips to town just to gamble.

Before he knew it, Tim was skipping school, and neglecting his family, friends, hobbies and homework so that he could spend more time gambling. Even when he was not gambling he was getting excited about the next chance he would get to go.

However, Tim was spending more than he was earning from his part-time job and his money was drying up. Tim felt that the arcade was the only place he was happy, so he started stealing money from his friends and from work to pay for his gambling. As Tim's gambling increased, his life started crumbling around him. He failed his exams, had problems keeping a steady job, and avoided his friends and family. Those around him knew that something was wrong but did not know what it was. Tim was very good at lying about his debts and lack of money, and creating excuses about where he had been.

Tim's gambling and stealing continued for years without anyone finding out until he was arrested for theft. At that point his life was shattered. His family and friends could not understand what had happened to him and found it difficult to cope. Getting caught made Tim face the fact that he had a problem. He started to see a counsellor to tackle his gambling addiction and help him piece his life back together. Although Tim has not gambled for over five years, he is scared of going back to gambling, and is still paying off his gambling debts.

Gambling and society

Whilst it might be right for governments to allow legal gambling so that it can be monitored, this has to be done carefully and with due consideration of its impact. In some countries, relaxed attitudes towards gambling have led to increases in numbers of people developing gambling problems.

Tolerance of gambling

A few years ago, Australia relaxed its laws on gambling and consequently people could walk into a hotel or club and gamble on high-payout video **lottery** machines. People could also go into any bar and choose between playing one of a number of gaming machines, or bet on the horses.

Australia now has the highest density of **slot machines** per person in the world. It was also the first country to venture down the road of **regulating** Internet gambling.

Making it worse?

This tolerance of gambling has had a number of social implications. The number of Australian people getting into trouble with gambling has risen sharply. Australia tops the league with a problem gambling **prevalence** rate of 2.3 per cent of the population. This has caused a number of Australian states to stop any further growth of gambling and to restrict access to, and numbers of, **pokie machines**.

Pokie machines have been linked to the significant rise in problem gamblers in Australia.

A learning process

Other countries are now learning from the experience of Australia. In 2002, for example, a government report on the future of gambling in the UK recommended the introduction of new gambling opportunities such as **e-gaming platforms**, changes in the current gambling law, as well as new legislation through the new Gambling Act. The report tells the gambling industry to run their businesses in a socially responsible fashion or risk losing their licences. This is a first for the UK since earlier legislation, with the exception of the National Lottery Act, has paid little regard to the social impact of gambling.

As more and more gambling opportunities become available, it is vital that safeguards are put in place to limit the number of people who lose control of their gambling.

43

Legal matters

Gambling is a cash-generating business. It is also an activity that, if mishandled, can cause enormous misery for the gamblers themselves and for those around them. Countries across the world need to control gambling with fairly tight regulations as a precaution against criminal exploitation, to prevent **money laundering**, and to protect children and the vulnerable from harm.

Age limits

The legal age at which a person is allowed to gamble varies from country to country, and even from state to state. In some states of the USA, for example, a person has to be eighteen to be able to gamble legally. In other states, the legal age is 25 for some types of gambling. In Australia, the legal age is usually eighteen. In the UK, a person can start gambling from the age of sixteen or eighteen, depending on the gambling activity.

Different countries also have other differences in law. For example, an underage gambler caught in the USA will be prosecuted and given a criminal conviction. In the UK and Australia, however, an underage gambler is not taken to court, but the **operator** may be. Operators caught allowing people under the legal age to gamble on their premises can have their gambling licence taken away.

Illegal gambling

Illegal gambling takes place in every country, even those where legal gambling is widely available. Sometimes the authorities will have a crackdown on illegal gambling activities. However, in too many instances the offenders are allowed to get away with it, as the hard-pressed police do not see gambling offences as a priority.

In some countries, the payment of gambling debts is not enforceable by law. For example, when someone who has been given credit by an operator loses and refuses to pay, there is nothing the operator can legally do to get their money back. The same rule applies when a gambler wins and finds that an operator refuses to pay out.

A lot of illegal betting takes place on the streets. During the soccer World Cup in 2002, people bet on the outcome of each football match.

Breaking the addiction

It is common for most gambling **addicts** to deny that they have a problem at all. They spend a lot of effort convincing themselves and others that they are in control of their gambling, and not responsible for any problems that their **addiction** may cause.

Hitting rock bottom

It often takes a crisis situation, such as a criminal conviction for theft, or the breakdown of a marriage, to force a gambler to face up to their problems and change. Whatever the trigger might be, the term that describes this point of desperation is 'rock bottom'. At this point, the life of the gambler, and often those around them, starts falling apart. Owning up to and addressing a gambling addiction is a very stressful experience. It can often tip the individual back into excessive gambling.

In extreme cases, problem gamblers may end up living on the streets.

❝I realized I had a problem after my firm gave me the sack when they discovered I was stealing from them. My world just fell apart and, for the first time, I realized I needed help.❞

(Anonymous problem gambler)

A man in China searches hopefully for an unused scratch card.

The road to recovery

It is important that the gambler has people that they can be honest with and turn to for support. The first issue that often causes the most stress is the mountain of debt that a lot of gamblers find themselves in. Working out a realistic plan to deal with the debts will help take the pressure off the individual and allow them to focus on other important issues.

The gambler has spent their gambling life lying and deceiving the people around them as well as themselves. It is important that they learn to be open and honest with family, friends and colleagues in order to establish a level of trust.

Although gambling addiction does not have the same strong physical **withdrawal symptoms** as drug abuse and alcoholism for example, there are still significant **psychological** withdrawal symptoms that the gambler may experience. They may have been using gambling to escape from pressure and depression, and to make themselves feel good. Without this crutch, they may well become tense, irritable and restless when under pressure. It is important that they find an alternative activity to be involved with whenever they feel the urge to gamble, otherwise it will be easy for them to start gambling again.

Treatment and counselling

Gambling **addiction** should be taken seriously. Most individuals will need to seek professional support. Since gambling has become more popular and accessible, many organizations have been established to provide help for those with a gambling problem.

Advice and support

Gambling is often a product of other issues within an individual's life. Counselling can be an effective method of addressing those issues. It may help the individual to understand what led to their gambling in the first place and to recognize the triggers that set them off into a gambling episode. Counselling has also been used to help the family of the problem gambler understand the situation and what they are going through.

Telephone helplines can provide valuable support for problem gamblers. Some helplines will suggest organizations where the gambler can get further help. Others offer a counselling service to gamblers and their families. Helplines can be an attractive option, especially for young people who do not feel ready for face to face counselling.

Residential homes for gamblers are also available. These homes are especially effective for those who have lost their own homes because of their gambling. They provide shelter as well as support and counselling for the individual, and can help them return back into society.

Self-help groups

Self-help groups are well established, and some gamblers find them useful and supportive. Gamblers Anonymous (GA) is the largest self-help group for problem gamblers. At GA meetings, a small group of ex-gamblers meets together to share experiences and common difficulties. The individuals in the group use each other for support and motivation to stop gambling.

Different methods of treatment and support will be effective for different people. Whilst some gamblers want to examine their own behaviour and reasons for gambling within a counselling environment, others will want to lean on other ex-gamblers for support within a self-help group.

Telephone helplines allow individuals to remain anonymous and talk about their problem in confidence.

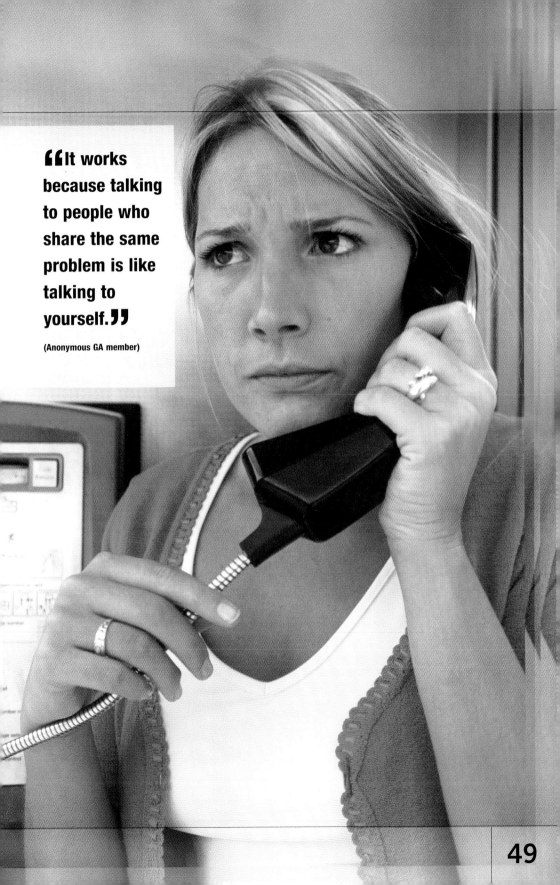

"It works because talking to people who share the same problem is like talking to yourself."

(Anonymous GA member)

Gambling with control

Gambling is an activity that the majority of the population can enjoy, but for a small minority it can turn into a damaging **addiction**. Whilst most people who have become addicted to gambling are able to overcome their problem through support and professional help, it is always safer to take steps to keep gambling under control.

Just for fun

Gambling can be fun and exciting, but it is always important to remember that it is a form of entertainment – not a way of making money. For the **operators**, gambling is a cash-generating business – they set the **odds** so that they will make money overall.

Most gamblers do lose. Being able to accept losing is an important part of keeping control – otherwise the gambler will become frustrated and spend more and more money in order to win back what they have lost.

Setting limits

Problems often start when a person spends more than they can afford. Setting strict limits on how much to spend on gambling is a good way of keeping control. For some people it is difficult to walk away from a gambling activity whether money has been won or lost – when it is lost, the temptation is to carry on to recover the losses; and when money is won it is tempting to try to win more. The best way to stay in control is being able to walk away at the right time. As already highlighted, gambling can seem to offer an escape from worries and pressure. However, this can be damaging and should be avoided.

Gambling addiction can be as damaging as any other addiction, but by being responsible about gambling and avoiding possible risks, many people are able to enjoy the experience, without harming themselves or others.

Gambling is still a popular form of entertainment that can be enjoyable if it is kept under control.

Information and advice

There are organizations that specialize in support, advice and counselling for problem gamblers. The following organizations will either advise on local projects or provide support and counselling themselves.

Problem gambling contacts in the UK

Gamblers Anonymous
Tel: 020 73843040
www.gamblersanonymous.org.uk
A self-help fellowship of compulsive gamblers wanting to address their gambling problems. Their sister organization, GamAnon, runs groups for partners and families of compulsive gamblers. Groups are held weekly throughout the country.

GamCare
Helpline: 0845 6000133
Suite 1, Catherine House,
25–27 Catherine Place, London SW1E 6DU
Tel: 020 7233 8988
www.gamcare.org.uk
A national helpline providing information, advice and counselling to individuals, their families and friends, who have concerns about problem gambling. GamCare also provides social education and literature, runs problem prevention and information programmes, and operates training courses and workshops. Local counselling services are also available dependent on location.

Gordon House Association
43–45 Maughan Street, Dudley,
West Midlands
DY1 2BA
Tel: 01384 241292
A hostel providing accommodation, therapy and rehabilitation for problem gamblers. A second hostel is based in Beckenham, South London.

Citizens Advice Bureaux (CAB)
The CAB offers debt counselling. Look in the local telephone directory for details.

North East Council on Addiction (NECA)
Philipson House, 5 Philipson Street, Walker, Newcastle upon Tyne NE6 4EN
Tel: 0191 2221262
www.neca.co.uk
All centres provide telephone and one-to-one counselling to problem gamblers and their relatives or friends. NECA has centres in Newcastle, South Tyne, Gateshead, Durham, Consett, Peterlee, Hartlepool, Washington, Stanley, Mid Tyne and Chester-le-Street.

National Debtline
Tel: 0808 8084000
www.nationaldebtline.co.uk
This organization offers advice and support to enable callers to deal with their debts in a pro-active and informal way. Self-help information packs are sent free to individuals with debt problems.

Contacts in Australia

G-Line
Tel: 1800 622112
www.g-line.org.au
This is a government-funded telephone crisis counselling and referral service for problem gamblers and anyone affected by their behaviour. It covers New South Wales, Victoria, Queensland and Western Australia.

Gamblers Anonymous
Helpline: (02) 9564-1574
www.gamblersanonymous.org.au
A self-help fellowship of compulsive gamblers wanting to address their gambling problems. Their sister organization, GamAnon, runs groups for partners/families of compulsive gamblers. Groups are held weekly throughout the country.

Contacts in New Zealand

New Zealand Problem Gambling Helpline
Tel: 0800 654 655
www.gamblingproblem.co.nz
This helpline offers over-the-phone counselling and referral to direct face-to-face counselling centres across New Zealand for problem gamblers and those affected by problem gambling. It also provides information and literature.

Further reading

Adolescent Gambling, by Mark Griffiths; Routledge, 1995

A Certain Bet? Exploring Gambling (GamCare leaflet); GamCare, 1997

Gambling – A Family Affair, by Angela Williams; Sheldon Press, 1996

Supporting a Problem Gambler: A Guide for Parents, Partners and Relatives (GamCare leaflet); GamCare, 2001

A Sure Bet: How to Control Your Gambling (GamCare leaflet); GamCare, 2001

Understanding Problem Gambling, by Paul Bellringer; Free Association Books, 1999

The Young Fruit Machine Player, by Dr Sue Fisher and Paul Bellringer; UK Forum on Young People and Gambling, 1994

Why Do People Gamble? by Kaye Stearman; Hodder Wayland, 2001

Glossary

absenteeism
frequent and continued absence from work or school

addict
a person who has a harmful habit, which they are unable to stop

addiction
a potentially dangerous habit that a person cannot control

addictive
an activity that a person may become hooked on

amusement arcades
enclosed areas or venues that contain fruit machines

anxieties
worries, fears and nervousness

betting office
a shop where bets are placed on the outcome of sporting or other events

bingo
a game of chance involving picking numbers

blackjack
the most popular card game in casinos, also known as pontoon or 21s

bookmaker
a company or person that accepts bets from the public on the outcome of events

casino
a public room or building where gambling takes place

craps
a casino game where gamblers place bets on the outcome of the roll of a pair of dice

dealer
a member of staff in a casino that works on the card tables, also known as a croupier

disorientation
loss of balance or sense of position

e-gaming platforms
electronic appliances used for gambling, such as computers, interactive TVs and mobile phones

federal law
law that is passed by a state and applies only to that state, rather than the whole country

form guides
lists of past performances of horses, dogs or teams in races or matches. Gamblers use this information to gauge how likely they are to win the next event.

fruit machines
popular gambling machines based on matching symbols on reels

full-house
a bingo term, used to describe the point when all the numbers featured on a person's card have been called out and they have won

jackpot
the maximum amount a person can win from a gambling activity

keno
a lottery-based game in Japan that involves picking winning numbers

lottery
a means of raising money by selling numbered tickets and giving prizes to the holders of numbers drawn at random

mental disorder
severe disturbances in a person's behaviour

money laundering
transferring funds to conceal an illegal act

Mormons
a religious group established in the USA in 1830.

obsession
a persistent idea or impulse

odds
a figure giving the chance or probability of a win for a certain event. The odds also indicate how much a person will win from a bet.

off-course betting
placing bets on races in a bookmaker's shop, rather than at a racecourse, which is on-course betting

operators
organizations running a gambling activity

pathological
unable to resist the need to carry out an activity

pokies
popular electronic poker machines

preoccupation
an obsession

prevalence
the frequency of a certain activity

prohibition
a ban on a certain activity by the state

psychological
to do with the mind

regulating
controlling an activity through governmental rules and restrictions

reservations
areas of land that are set aside for a specific purpose or group of people

roulette
a popular casino game of chance, where bets are placed on the number upon which a ball will land on a spinning wheel

scratch cards
special cards coated in a waxy substance that may be scratched off to reveal whether or not a prize has been won

slot machines
another name for a fruit machine

spread betting
a higher-risk form of betting on sports events and stocks and shares. The customer bets on whether a result will be higher or lower than the prediction that is set by the operator. The amount won or lost depends on how much higher or lower the result is.

stake
the amount bet by a gambler on a single bet

vice
an activity that is seen by society as immoral

virtual casinos
casinos that are based on the Internet or interactive TV

withdrawal symptoms
uncomfortable physical and mental feelings experienced by a person after stopping an addiction

Index

Titles in the *Need to Know* series include:

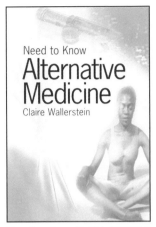

Need to Know
Alternative Medicine
Claire Wallerstein

Hardback   0 431 09808 5

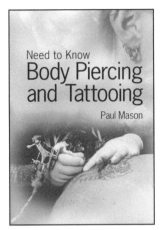

Need to Know
Body Piercing and Tattooing
Paul Mason

Hardback   0 431 09818 2

Need to Know
Depression
Claire Wallerstein

Hardback   0 431 09809 3

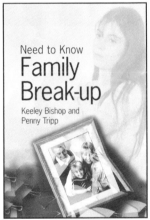

Need to Know
Family Break-up
Keeley Bishop and Penny Tripp

Hardback   0 431 09810 7

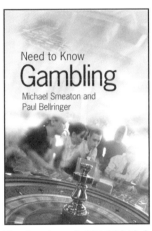

Need to Know
Gambling
Michael Smeaton and Paul Bellringer

Hardback   0 431 09819 0

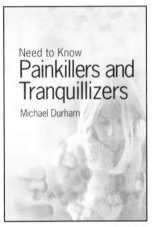

Need to Know
Painkillers and Tranquillizers
Michael Durham

Hardback   0 431 09811 5

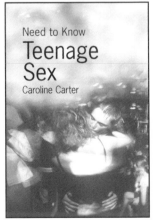

Need to Know
Teenage Sex
Caroline Carter

Hardback   0 431 09821 2

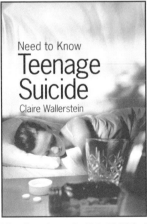

Need to Know
Teenage Suicide
Claire Wallerstein

Hardback   0 431 09820 4

Find out about the other titles in this series on our website www.heinemann.co.uk/library